ISAAC ASIMOV'S NEW LIBRARY OF THE UNIVERSE

THE RED PLANET: MARS

BY ISAAC ASIMOV
WITH REVISIONS AND UPDATING BY FRANCIS REDDY

Gareth Stevens Publishing
MILWAUKEE

For a free color catalog describing Gareth Stevens' list of high-quality books, call 1-800-542-2595 (USA) or 1-800-461-9120 (Canada). Gareth Stevens' Fax: (414) 225-0377.

A special thanks to Gina Nelson (Jet Propulsion Laboratory) and Jody Swann (United States Geological Survey).

Library of Congress Cataloging-in-Publication Data

Asimov, Isaac.
    The red planet: Mars / by Isaac Asimov and Francis Reddy.
       p. cm. — (Isaac Asimov's New library of the universe)
    Rev. ed. of: Mars: our mysterious neighbor. 1988.
    Includes index.
    ISBN 0-8368-1132-1
    1. Mars (Planet)—Juvenile literature. [1. Mars (Planet).
  2. Planets.] I. Reddy, Francis, 1959-. II. Asimov, Isaac.
  Mars: our mysterious neighbor. III. Title. IV. Series:
  Asimov, Isaac. New library of the universe.
  QB641.A755 1994
  523.4'3—dc20   94-15425

This edition first published in 1994 by
Gareth Stevens Publishing
1555 North RiverCenter Drive, Suite 201
Milwaukee, Wisconsin 53212, USA

Revised and updated edition © 1994 by Gareth Stevens, Inc. Original edition published in 1988 by Gareth Stevens, Inc., under the title *Mars: Our Mysterious Neighbor.* Text © 1994 by Nightfall, Inc. End matter and revisions © 1994 by Gareth Stevens, Inc.

Project editor: Barbara J. Behm
Design adaptation: Helene Feider
Editorial assistant: Diane Laska
Production director: Susan Ashley
Picture research: Kathy Keller
Artwork commissioning: Kathy Keller and Laurie Shock
Research editor: Scott Enk

Printed in the United States of America

2 3 4 5 6 7 8 9 99 98 97 96 95

To bring this classic of young people's information up to date, the editors at Gareth Stevens Publishing have selected two noted science authors, Greg Walz-Chojnacki and Francis Reddy. Walz-Chojnacki and Reddy coauthored the recent book *Celestial Delights: The Best Astronomical Events Through 2001.*

Walz-Chojnacki is also the author of the book *Comet: The Story Behind Halley's Comet* and various articles about the space program. He was an editor of *Odyssey,* an astronomy and space technology magazine for young people, for eleven years.

Reddy is the author of nine books, including *Halley's Comet, Children's Atlas of the Universe, Children's Atlas of Earth Through Time,* and *Children's Atlas of Native Americans,* plus numerous articles. He was an editor of *Astronomy* magazine for several years.

CONTENTS

Is There Life on Mars? 5
A Struggle for Survival 6
A Dead World? 9
Another Look 10
Probing Mars 13
No Life as We Know It 14
Captured Moons 17
Getting There Is Half the Fun 18
A Global Effort 21
Futuristic Colonies 23
Challenging Exploration 24
Terraforming Mars 27
Two Moons of Mars 28
Mars versus Earth 28
Fact File: Mars Revealed 29

More Books about Mars 30
Video 30
Places to Visit 30
Places to Write 30
Glossary 31
Index 32

We live in an enormously large place – the Universe. It's only in the last fifty-five years or so that we've found out how large it probably is. It's only natural that we would want to understand the place in which we live, so scientists have developed instruments – such as radio telescopes, satellites, probes, and many more – that have told us far more about the Universe than could possibly be imagined.

We have seen planets up close. We have learned about quasars and pulsars, black holes, and supernovas. We have gathered amazing data about how the Universe may have come into being and how it may end. Nothing could be more astonishing.

But not everything we see in the sky is brand new. Thousands of years ago, people watched the sky and noticed that certain bright stars shifted position from night to night. The Greeks called them "wandering stars." Naturally, they called them that using the Greek language. Their words have come down to us to mean "planet." One of these planets has a reddish color, almost the color of blood. It was, therefore, named after the god of war, Mars. In this book, you will learn what scientists have discovered about the fascinating planet Mars.

Isaac Asimov

Above: When astronauts of the future first orbit Mars, a view like this will greet them. Computers combined many *Viking Orbiter* images to create this view of Mars as seen from the window of a spacecraft 1,500 miles (2,500 kilometers) above the Red Planet. Near the center is the crater Schiaparelli, about 280 miles (450 km) across. Frost fills craters and dusts the landscape at lower right.

Is There Life on Mars?

Let's leave Earth, heading away from the Sun. Mars is the first planet we see. What do we know about our neighbor, Mars? We know quite a bit, but Mars is a mysterious planet, too. We know that it is smaller than Earth. It is only half as wide as Earth, and it has only one-tenth Earth's mass. Still, Mars turns, or rotates, once every 24-1/2 hours. Its axis is tipped so that it has seasons like Earth's. Mars is colder, though, because it is farther from the Sun. It has ice caps at the poles. Of all the planets in our Solar System, it is the one most like Earth. So, in the past, people wondered if there were living creatures on Mars. If so, what were they like? This was the big mystery of Mars.

Below: Although this color-enhanced picture from the *Viking 2* lander has little scientific value, it captures our imagination. When will humans view a Martian sunrise with their own eyes?

A Struggle for Survival

We know that living creatures would have a hard time surviving on Mars. Early astronomers could tell that it had only a thin atmosphere, very little water, and was probably made up of a large desert. In 1877, however, narrow, dark markings were seen on Mars. These were studied by an American astronomer, Percival Lowell. He thought they were canals, dug by intelligent Martians to bring water from the ice caps at the poles to the desert areas on the rest of Mars. Lowell wrote several books on the subject. And, for a while, many people were sure there was intelligent life on Mars.

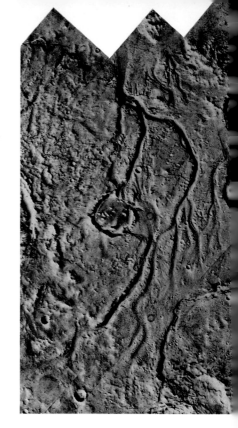

Above: These channels on Mars may have been carved by water long ago. They are not the same as the ones seen by Lowell, which may have been an optical illusion.

Opposite, top: Percival Lowell in a 1905 photograph. He is looking at Venus by daylight through a telescope that has been in continuous use since 1897.

Opposite, bottom: Percival Lowell plotted, on globes of Mars, the "canals" and "lakes" he believed he saw on Mars.

! *Calling all Martians!*

People were once so sure Mars had intelligent beings on it that ways were invented to send them messages. One scientist suggested that huge triangles and squares be dug in Siberia, filled with oil, and set on fire at night. The Martians would see these through their telescopes, and then they might arrange something for us to see in return. In 1938, the actor Orson Welles presented a fictional radio play in which Martians were said to be invading New Jersey. He frightened hundreds of listeners who got into their cars and drove away to escape the Martians — who really didn't exist.

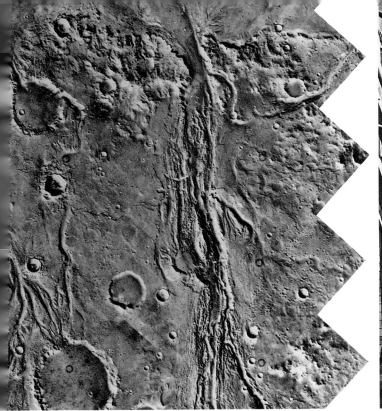

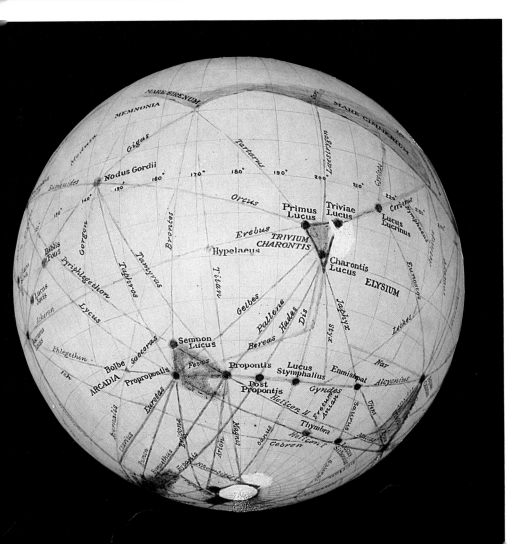

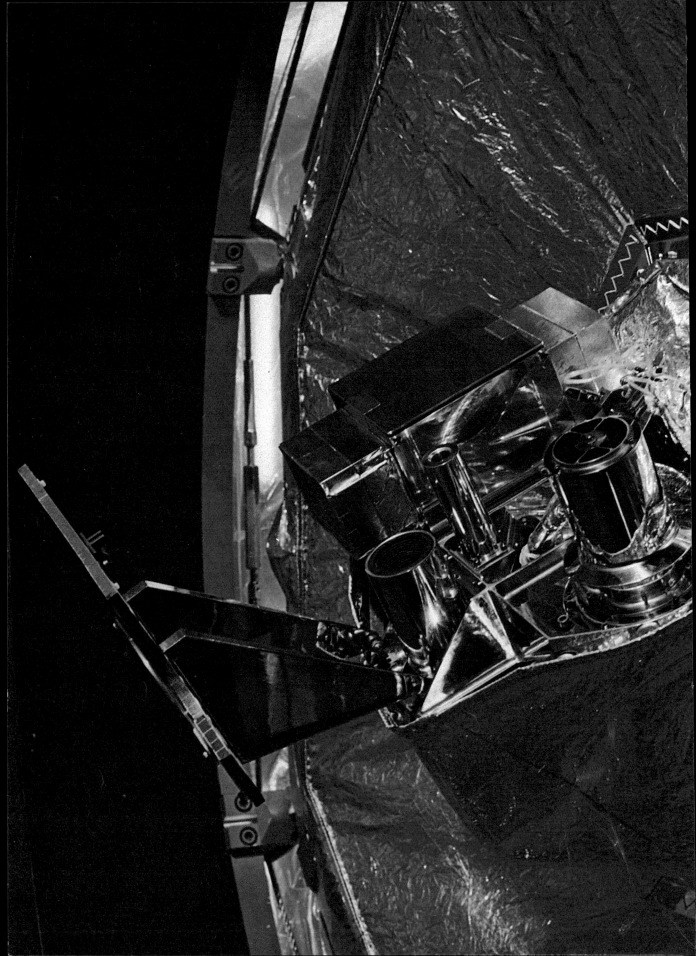

A Dead World?

For many years, people thought about the possibility of life on Mars. Finally, when scientists sent rockets to the planet, it seemed we would get some answers. In 1964, a probe, *Mariner 4*, was sent to Mars. In July, 1965, this probe passed within 6,000 miles (9,600 km) of Mars and took nineteen close-up photographs that it beamed back to Earth. These photographs showed craters on Mars like those on the Moon. Mars's atmosphere turned out to be only 1/100 as thick as Earth's, and there was no sign of any canals. Mars seemed to be a dead world.

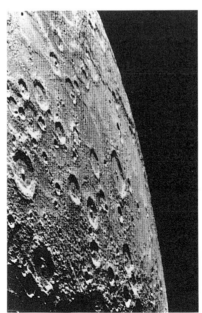

Far left: The *Mariner 4* television camera took pictures as it passed Mars, stored them on tape, and beamed them back to Earth. Each picture took about eight hours to play back, or reconstruct, from the radio transmission. The entire transmission lasted over seven days!

Left: The moonlike southern region of Mars. After years of thinking about the possibility of life on Mars, scientists know it is not likely. Many people were relieved, but others were disappointed. How do you feel about it? Would you have liked to meet Martians?

Another Look

In 1971, another Mars probe, *Mariner 9*, reached Mars. It went into orbit around Mars and took several photographs. It mapped almost the entire planet. There were definitely no canals. The photos showed that straight, dark lines, thought to be canals, were just illusions. The photos also showed many craters plus flat areas with extinct volcanoes on Mars. One of these volcanoes, Olympus Mons, was far larger than any volcano on Earth. The pictures also showed a huge canyon, named Valles Marineris, that was far larger than our own Grand Canyon. Mars's surface proved to be much more interesting than that of our Moon. But Mars still seemed to be a dead world.

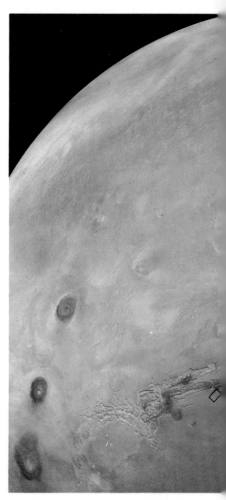

? *Mars — fooling the pros*

Why did Percival Lowell see canals on Mars when there weren't any? He was a good astronomer with excellent telescopes. He worked on high ground in Arizona where the air was very clear. It's possible that he could just barely see little dark patches on Mars.

His eyes, not knowing what to make of the patches, saw them as straight lines. During a scientific experiment, children looked at distant circles with little dark patches. The children saw straight lines – an optical illusion. Maybe that's what Lowell experienced.

Left, top: Over 3,100 miles (5,000 km) long and up to 5 miles (8 km) deep, the Valles Marineris dwarfs any canyon system on Earth. The tiny box pictured could include Earth's entire Grand Canyon. The three dark spots are Martian volcanoes. The crater of the bottom volcano, named Arsia Mons, is filled with fog.

Left, bottom: Olympus Mons, Mars's extinct volcano, is the largest known volcano in the Solar System. A *Viking* probe took this false-color image.

Below, right: Earth is not the only place in the Solar System where the weather can become violent. Mars is famous for its dust storms. Here's what a dust storm might look like from the floor of Valles Marineris.

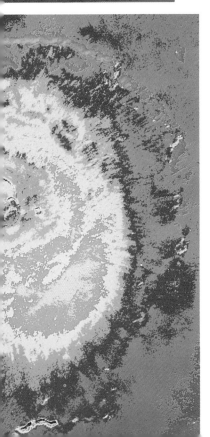

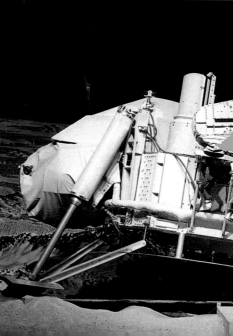

Probing Mars

In 1976, two new Mars probes, *Viking 1* and *Viking 2,* successfully put landers on the Martian surface. A part of the mission was to analyze the atmosphere of Mars. It was found to be about 95 percent carbon dioxide, and most of the rest is nitrogen and argon. This means that the Martian atmosphere has almost no oxygen in it. What's more, the Martian surface is as cold or colder than Antarctica. So any water on Mars must be frozen.

Opposite, top: Olympus Mons is about 15 miles (24 km) high — three times higher than the tallest mountain on Earth!

Opposite, bottom: The *back row* shows the peaks on Mars. Olympus Mons *(back, right)* is 86,618 feet (26,400 m) high. *Center row, left to right:* Earth's Mt. Everest (29,028 ft/8,848 m), Mt. Rainier (14,413 ft/4,393 m), and Mont Blanc (15,771 ft/ 4,807 m). *Front row:* Earth's Mt. Fuji (12,388 ft/ 3,776 m) and Mt. St. Helens (9,679 ft/ 2,950 m).

Below: The *Viking* test lander. The front footpad of this model rests on a rock, as the actual lander did on Mars. As a result, cameras in the lander showed the Martian horizon to be sloped. In fact, it is nearly perfectly level.

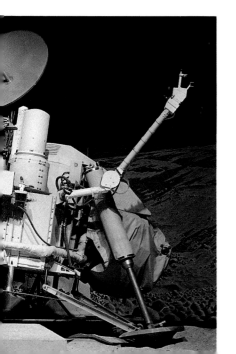

? More strange markings

The Mars probes have discovered strange markings on Mars. These markings look like dry river channels that run crookedly across the surface as real rivers would. Smaller channels run into larger ones just as smaller rivers run into larger ones on Earth. It seems almost certain that at one time in the past, Mars had water that formed rivers and, perhaps, lakes. In that case, what happened to the water? Is it now all frozen in the soil? And if Mars once had water, was the atmosphere thicker then, and was there life on Mars then? Scientists do not know.

No Life as We Know It

The *Viking* probes took photographs of Mars's surface and tested the Martian soil. If the soil contained microscopic forms of life, the tests would show the presence of chemical changes. The probes scooped up soil and tested it in three different ways to see if such changes took place. There were changes, but scientists were not certain that these changes were evidence of life. However, nothing was detected in the soil that contained carbon, which is essential to life as we know it. The surface of Mars may be more interesting than that of our Moon, but Mars may still truly be a dead world.

Above: The Martian horizon as photographed by the *Viking* lander. The lower center of this shot shows trenches left by the lander's sampling tools.

Opposite: The surface of Mars looks like a rocky desert like those found on Earth. The probes scooped samples of Martian soil for testing. None of the tests showed any signs of life as we know it.

Right: Another view of Mars from the Viking lander.

Captured Moons

Mars has two small satellites, or moons, called Phobos and Deimos. They may be captured satellites that were once passing Mars and were drawn into orbit by Mars's gravitational field. They are not large globes like our own Moon. From Earth, they look like two dim dots of light, but probes have shown them more clearly. They are shaped like potatoes and are covered with craters. Phobos is 17 miles (27 km) across at its longest point. Deimos is only 10 miles (16 km) across. Because of their small size and their closeness to Mars, these little satellites were not discovered until 1877. This was long after the more distant, but larger, satellites of Jupiter and Saturn were discovered.

! *If at first you don't succeed . . .*

The Martian satellites were discovered by an American astronomer named Asaph Hall. Night after night in 1877, he looked through his telescope at the space near Mars and could find nothing. Finally, he made up his mind that it was no use. He told his wife, whose maiden name was Stickney, that he was giving up. His wife said, "Try it one more night." He did and found the satellites. Now the largest crater on the Phobos satellite is named "Stickney" in honor of the woman who urged Hall not to give up.

Opposite: Martian moons. Top: Deimos. Bottom: Phobos. Deimos orbits Mars in about 30 hours. Phobos orbits Mars in about 7 hours and 40 minutes.

Top: The 1989 Soviet Phobos mission. One of the mission's goals was to drop landers on Phobos to map its surface and subsurface and to study this moon's composition.

Bottom: Viking 1 took pictures that were combined to create this image of Phobos. The craters pictured were probably caused by the impact of space debris.

Getting There Is Half the Fun

Exploration of Mars with spacecraft has been going on for more than thirty years. In that time, the United States has sent nine probes to Mars, and the former Soviet Union has sent ten. Yet of all the spacecraft launched toward the Red Planet, all but seven missions have failed in some important way. Many probes, including two of the last three launched, just stopped sending signals before even reaching the planet. Mars seems to be bad luck to spacecraft! Many ambitious Mars missions are planned for the coming years. The next mission, called MESUR Pathfinder, is scheduled for launch in 1996. If all goes according to plan, a probe will land on the Martian surface and send out a small-wheeled vehicle called a rover. Later, in 2000 and 2001, many similar robot visitors will explore different regions of Mars.

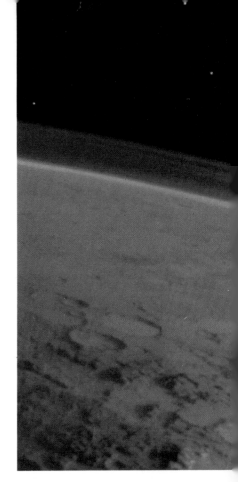

Top: Mars Observer was to be a grand return to Mars exploration, but it fell silent just before entering orbit.

Bottom: The *Viking* landers could only show us the Martian surface from one point. But in the next decade, a new generation of landers will bring along vehicles like this. They will be able to drive across the landscape and take pictures from different perspectives.

Probe	Launched	Country	Mission Summary
Mars 1	1962	*Former* U.S.S.R.	Failure: Probe failed before reaching Mars.
Mariner 3	1964	U.S.	Failure: Batteries died shortly after launch.
Mariner 4	1964	U.S.	Success! Mars flyby.
Zond 2	1964	U.S.S.R.	Failure: Probe failed before reaching Mars.
Mariner 6	1969	U.S.	Success! Mars flyby.
Mariner 7	1969	U.S.	Success! Mars flyby.
Mariner 8	1971	U.S.	Failure. Booster failed. Never reached orbit.
Mariner 9	1971	U.S.	Success! First to orbit Mars, first close-up images of Mars's moons.
Mars 2	1971	U.S.S.R.	Failure: Lander crashed on Mars.
Mars 3	1971	U.S.S.R.	Failure: Probe landed on Mars but stopped sending signals after just ninety seconds.
Mars 4	1973	U.S.S.R.	Failure: Reached Mars but failed to enter orbit.
Mars 5	1973	U.S.S.R.	Success! Returned images similar to those from *Mariner 9*.
Mars 6	1973	U.S.S.R.	Failure: Lander crashed.
Mars 7	1973	U.S.S.R.	Failure: Lander missed Mars.
Viking 1	1975	U.S.	Success! First images of Martian surface; chemical analysis of soil; search for life.
Viking 2	1975	U.S.	Success! First detection of Martian earthquake; mission similar to that of *Viking 1*.
Phobos 1	1988	U.S.S.R.	Failure: First attempt to land probes on Martian moon Phobos. Probe failed before reaching Mars.
Phobos 2	1988	U.S.S.R.	Failure: Signals ceased one week before Phobos landing.
Mars Observer	1992	U.S.	Failure: Contact lost just before achieving Mars orbit.

Above: A Martian scorecard.
So far, our exploration of the Red
Planet has had mixed success.

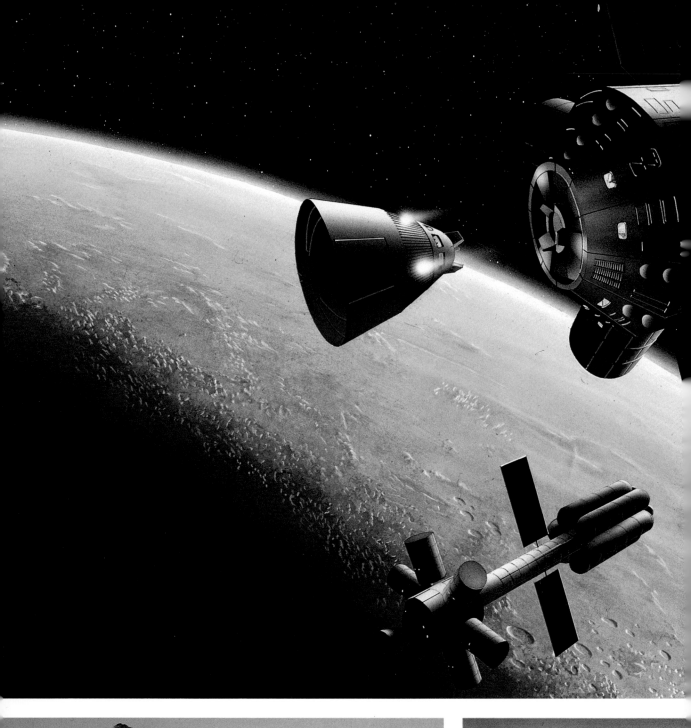

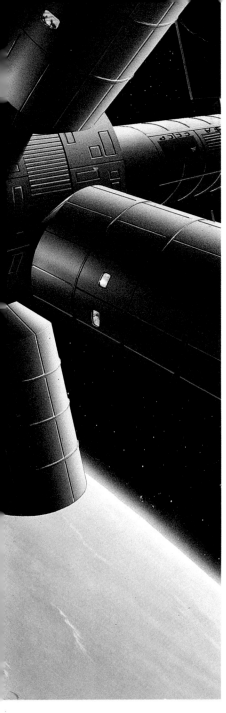

A Global Effort

Think of how much we'd still be wondering about Mars if not for amazing probes like *Mariner* and *Viking*. But no matter how wonderful these probes might be, we could do so much more if spaceships carried astronauts to Mars. This would not be an easy task because it might take nearly two years for such a mission to return to Earth. Some people think this would be too big a job for any one nation. Perhaps the United States and Russia, working together, could send a combined expedition to Mars. They could explore our mysterious neighbor and study its craters, canyons, volcanoes, ice caps, and other interesting features they may find. What they learn may help us better understand our own planet.

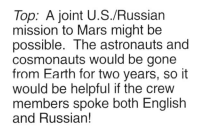

Top: A joint U.S./Russian mission to Mars might be possible. The astronauts and cosmonauts would be gone from Earth for two years, so it would be helpful if the crew members spoke both English and Russian!

Left: Fog in a Martian canyon. In the background are ice-covered mountains. Nothing is liquid on Mars at present, although there may once have been water there.

Opposite, bottom: A beautiful watchtower formation at Kasei Vallis, Mars. This scenery might make a two-year trip to Mars worthwhile for someone who really loves to travel.

21

Futuristic Colonies

What else might we do if we were able to send people to Mars? We can imagine colonies on the Moon, since the Moon is only three days' rocket-time away from Earth. Mars is much farther away, but in some ways it is an easier world to live on than our Moon. Mars has a gravitational pull that is 2/5 that of Earth, while the Moon's is only 1/6 that of Earth. Mars has a thin atmosphere that can protect people from meteors and radiation a bit, while the Moon has none. Mars has polar ice that could be used for water, while the Moon does not. We can imagine cities built underground on Mars, or perhaps domed cities on its surface. And if we count the Moon, humans will then be living on three different worlds.

Left: To explorers stationed on Phobos, Mars would loom large and red.

Inset, top: A futuristic colony on Mars would have an artificial environment — inside buildings, space suits, and vehicles — making the Martian atmosphere fit for humans. Landing at the colony would be easy enough, and the rocket launch site would allow people to leave as well.

Inset, bottom: A mission carrying people flies past Phobos on its way to Mars. The orbit of Phobos carries it about 6,000 miles (9,600 km) above the surface of the Red Planet. The tiny moon may play an important role in future missions to place humans on Mars.

Challenging Exploration

What would space explorers do on Mars? Once settlements are established on Mars, exploration parties can be sent out. Imagine the explorers in special cars, driving along the bottom of a canyon that stretches for 3,000 miles (4,800 km). Imagine a party climbing a giant volcano and studying the inside of the crater. Think of explorers making their way across the Martian ice caps at its poles. We know the ice caps contain frozen carbon dioxide as well as frozen water. But we could learn even more about Mars from the ice caps. We might find interesting minerals or even matter that will help us understand what Mars was like millions of years ago.

? The moons of Mars — a clue to life on Earth?

Phobos and Deimos don't look like Mars. Mars has a light reddish surface, but Phobos and Deimos have dark surfaces. That is probably because the satellites were once asteroids. There are certain dark meteorites that occasionally land on Earth. They contain small amounts of water and carbon-containing compounds that somewhat resemble those found in living things. Maybe it would be more interesting to study the surfaces of Mars's satellites than to study Mars. This might help us investigate how life originated on Earth.

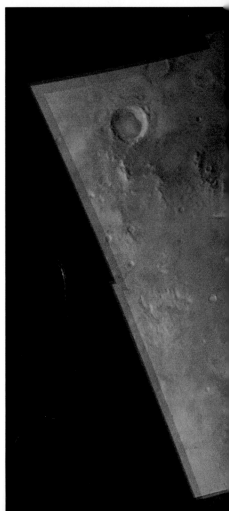

Top: When human beings land on Mars, they can explore the insides of inactive volcanoes like this one — the Hecates Tholus Lava Tube.

Bottom: The south pole of Mars has something in common with Earth's South Pole — ice!

Opposite: Glaciers of ice crawl across the Martian surface. Millions of years ago, creeping glaciers formed the hills and valleys of Earth with the same slow, relentless movement.

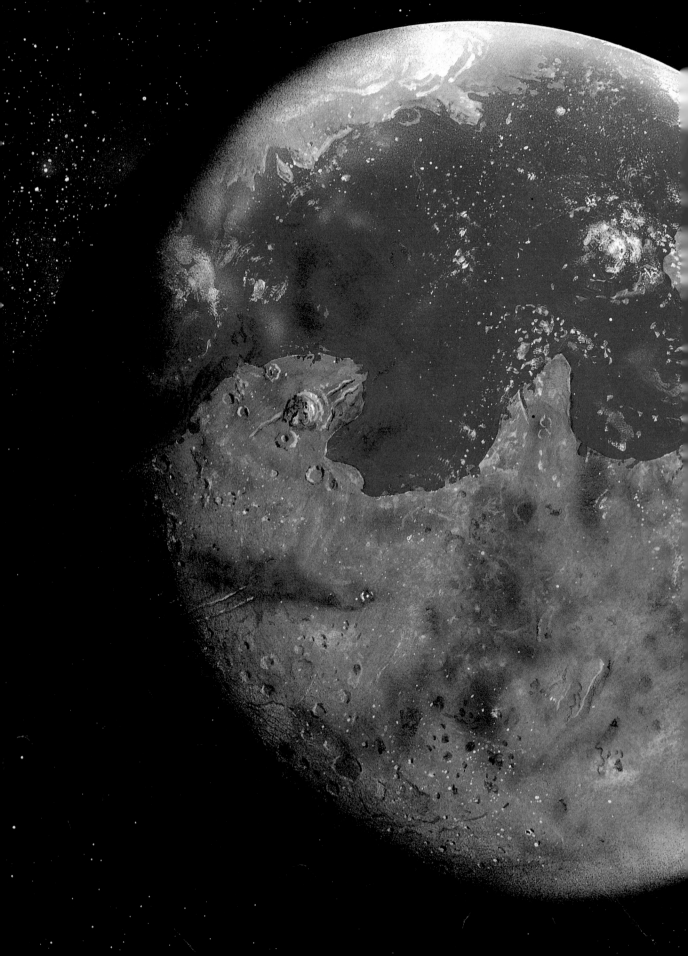

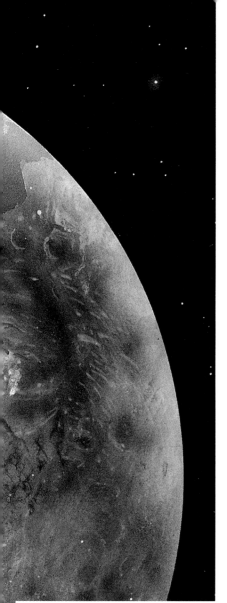

Terraforming Mars

Even more exciting activities might be possible on Mars. The early settlers on Mars might be able to alter certain conditions to make the planet more like Earth. This is called terraforming. Perhaps large supplies of water could be brought in from the asteroids. If the right gases were added to the atmosphere, Mars would trap more sunlight and become warmer. In that case, the water would not freeze but would form an ocean. Enough oxygen might be added to make the air breathable. Many plants and animals could then be brought to Mars. It may take many, many years; but perhaps Mars can someday become a little Earth.

Left: Here's a hot idea for the future: If we altered the climate and atmosphere of Mars by terraforming, we could melt the northern ice cap to create an ocean.

Inset: On a terraformed Mars, humans would not have to depend on artificial devices to breathe, keep warm or cool, or supply themselves with water. The terraformed climate would sustain human life "naturally."

Two Moons of Mars

Name	Diameter	Distance from Mars's Center
Phobos	13-18 miles (20-28 km)	5,827 miles (9,378 km)
Deimos	6-10 miles (10-16 km)	14,577 miles (23,459 km)

Mars versus Earth

Planet	Diameter	Rotation Period (length of day)	Period of Orbit around Sun (length of year)	Known Moons	Surface Gravity	Distance from Sun (nearest-farthest)	Least Time for Light to Travel to Earth
Mars	4,217 miles (6,786 km)	24 hours, 37 minutes	687 days (1.88 years)	2	0.38*	129-155 million miles (207-249 million km)	3.1 minutes
Earth	7,927 miles (12,756 km)	23 hours, 56 minutes	365.25 days (one year)	1	–	91-94 million miles (147-152 million km)	–

* Multiply your weight by this number to find out how much you would weigh on this planet.

Fact File: Mars Revealed

Above: The Sun and its Solar System family, *left to right*: Mercury, Venus, Earth, Mars, Jupiter, Saturn, Uranus, Neptune, and Pluto.

Inset: A close-up of Mars and its two tiny satellites, Phobos *(top)* and Deimos *(bottom)*.

Mars is the seventh largest planet (Earth is fifth), the fourth closest to the Sun, and the first planet beyond Earth's orbit. It is also, therefore, the last of the "inner" group of planets, all of which are within what is known as the asteroid belt. Beyond the asteroids is the "outer" group that begins with Jupiter. With an axial tilt similar to Earth's and a day that is virtually the same length as ours, Mars has the same type of seasons as Earth. Of course, Mars is much farther from the Sun than Earth is, so Mars has a longer "year" than we do. Its seasons are much longer, and its temperatures are much colder than Earth's.

More Books about Mars

Exploring Outer Space: Rockets, Probes, and Satellites. Asimov (Gareth Stevens)
Maria Looney on the Red Planet. Beatty (Avon)
Mars and the Inner Planets. Vogt (Franklin Watts)
Miss Pickerell Goes to Mars. MacGregor (Archway)
Our Planetary System. Asimov (Gareth Stevens)
Planets. Barrett (Franklin Watts)

Video

Mars: Our Mysterious Neighbor. (Gareth Stevens)

Places to Visit

You can explore Mars and other parts of the Universe without leaving Earth. Here are some museums and centers where you can find a variety of space exhibits.

NASA Lewis Research Center
Educational Services Office
21000 Brookpark Road
Cleveland, OH 44135

NASA Goddard Space Flight Center
Greenbelt Road
Greenbelt, MD 20771

Astrocentre
Royal Ontario Museum
100 Queen's Park
Toronto, Ontario M5S 2C6

Henry Crown Science Center
Museum of Science and Industry
57th Street and Lake Shore Drive
Chicago, IL 60637

Edmonton Space and Science Centre
11211 - 142nd Street
Edmonton, Alberta K5M 4A1

Australian Museum
6-8 College Street
Sydney, NSW 2000 Australia

Places to Write

Here are some places you can write for more information about Mars. Be sure to state what kind of information you would like. Include your full name and address so they can write back to you.

National Space Society
922 Pennsylvania Avenue, SE
Washington, D.C. 20003

NASA Kennedy Space Center
PA-ESB
Kennedy Space Center, FL 32899

Jet Propulsion Laboratory
Public Affairs 180-201
4800 Oak Grove Drive
Pasadena, CA 91109

Sydney Observatory
P.O. Box K346
Haymarket 2000 Australia

Glossary

asteroids: very small "planets" made of rock or metal. There are thousands of them in our Solar System, and they mainly orbit the Sun between Mars and Jupiter. Some show up elsewhere in the Solar System, however, and many scientists think the two moons of Mars are really "captured" asteroids.

atmosphere: the gases that surround a planet.

axis: the imaginary line through the center of a planet around which the planet rotates. The axis of Mars is tipped so that its seasons change as the planet orbits the Sun.

canal: a river or waterway made by people to move water from one place to another. It was once thought that the narrow, dark markings on Mars were canals built by Martians to move water from the ice caps to the desert areas.

carbon dioxide: a heavy, colorless gas that makes up 95 percent of the Martian atmosphere. When humans and other animals breathe, they exhale carbon dioxide.

colonies: human settlements. Many people have wondered if it might be possible to one day set up colonies on Mars.

craters: holes on planets and moons created by volcanic activity or the impact of meteorites.

desert: a waterless area on land. Mars is often considered a desert planet.

extinct: no longer living or active. Both the dinosaurs and inactive volcanoes are said to be extinct.

ice cap: a cover of permanent ice at either or both ends of a planet. Mars has ice caps at both ends.

Mars: the god of war in mythology. The planet Mars is named for him.

mass: a quantity, or amount, of matter.

Olympus Mons: a huge, extinct volcano on Mars.

planet: one of the bodies that revolves around our Sun. Earth is one of the planets, and so is Mars.

satellite: a smaller body orbiting a larger body. Phobos and Deimos are Mars's natural satellites, or moons. *Sputnik 1* and *2* were Earth's first artificial satellites.

terraforming: a way of making a planet suitable for human life.

Valles Marineris: an enormous canyon on Mars.

Viking 1 and 2: probes that actually landed on Mars and sent back information about the planet to Earth.

Index

Antarctica 13
argon 13
Arizona 10
Arsia Mons 10-11
asteroid belt 29
asteroids 24, 27
astronauts 21

canals on Mars 6-7, 9, 10
carbon 14, 24
carbon dioxide 13, 24
cosmonauts 21
craters 4, 9, 10-11, 16-17, 21, 24

Deimos 16-17, 24, 28-29

Earth 5, 8-9, 10-11, 12-13, 14-15, 17, 20-21, 23, 24-25, 27, 29

glaciers 24-25
Grand Canyon 10-11
gravity and gravitational field 17, 23

Hall, Asaph 17
Hecates Tholus Lava Tube 24-25

Jupiter 17, 29

Kasei Vallis 20-21

Lowell, Percival 6-7, 10

Mariner probes 8-9, 10, 21
Mars mission, joint U.S./Russia 20-21
Mars Observer 18-19
Martians 6, 9

MESUR Pathfinder 18
Moon, Earth's 9, 10, 14, 17, 23
moons of Mars (*see* Deimos *and* Phobos)

nitrogen 13

Olympus Mons 10-11, 12-13
oxygen 13, 27

Phobos 16-17, 22-23, 24, 28-29
polar ice caps, Martian 5, 6-7, 21, 24, 27

rover 18-19

Saturn 17
Schiaparelli 4
seasons on Mars 5, 29
Siberia 6
Solar System 5, 11, 28-29
South Pole 24-25
Soviet Union (former) 16-17, 18-19
Stickney 17

terraforming 26-27

United States 18-19, 21

Valles Marineris 10-11
Venus 6-7
Viking probes 4-5, 10-11, 12-13, 14-15, 16-17, 18-19, 21
volcanoes 10-11, 21, 24

Welles, Orson 6

Born in 1920, Isaac Asimov came to the United States as a young boy from his native Russia. As a young man, he was a student of biochemistry. In time, he became one of the most productive writers the world has ever known. His books cover a spectrum of topics, including science, history, language theory, fantasy, and science fiction. His brilliant imagination gained him the respect and admiration of adults and children alike. Sadly, Isaac Asimov died shortly after the publication of the first edition of *Isaac Asimov's Library of the Universe*.

The publishers wish to thank the following for permission to reproduce copyright material: front cover, © Doug McLeod 1987; 4, United States Geological Survey; 5, National Space Science Data Center; 6-7, Jet Propulsion Laboratory; 7 (upper and lower), Lowell Observatory; 8-9, NASA; 9, Jet Propulsion Laboratory; 10-11 (upper), United States Geological Survey; 10-11 (lower), NASA; 11, © John Foster 1988; 12 (upper), United States Geological Survey; 12 (lower), © John Waite 1987; 12-13, 14, NASA; 14-15, National Space Science Data Center; 15, 16, NASA; 16-17 (upper), © Michael Carroll 1987; 16-17 (lower), Jet Propulsion Laboratory; 18-19 (upper), NASA; 18-19 (lower), Jet Propulsion Laboratory; 20, © MariLynn Flynn 1987; 20-21 (upper), © Doug McLeod 1987; 20-21 (lower), © David Hardy; 22 (upper), © Ron Miller 1987; 22 (lower), © Paul DiMare 1985; 22-23, © MariLynn Flynn 1985; 24-25 (upper), © MariLynn Flynn 1987; 24-25 (lower), United States Geological Survey; 25, © Michael Carroll 1987; 26-27, © Michael Carroll 1985; 27, © Julian Baum 1988; 28-29 (all), © Sally Bensusen 1987.